I0190483

My Wife
Is the Pastor

JERALD W. FLOWERS, SR.

Llumina
Christian
Books

Unless otherwise indicated, all scripture quotations are from the King James Version of the Bible.

MY WIFE IS THE PASTOR
ISBN: 16255039-5-4
COPYRIGHT 2012 BY JERALD WAYNE FLOWERS, SR.

PUBLISHED BY J.T. FLOWERS
P.O. BOX 671522
HOUSTON, TX 77267-1522

FIRST PRINTING 2012

ISBN: 978-1-62550-395-4

Printed in the United States of America by Llumina Press

Contents

Dedication

This book is dedicated to the Body of Christ as a strengthening tool to help validate the truth: God is no respecter of gender or persons in the operation of the local church.

I further dedicate this book to my wife, J.T. Flowers, who is a called woman of God serving as Pastor of Time of Celebration Ministries Church in Houston, Texas. I highly recommend every female in the Body of Christ to read this book. The intent is to reveal the truth from God's perspective about women in ministry, particularly female pastors, and what the Word of God really says about this very controversial subject.

Finally, I dedicate this book to Renada McKnight, Ashleigh McCall and Sharon Boyd. I am especially grateful for their editing and proofreading skills in the production of this book.

Hebrews 6:10 KJV
For God is not unrighteous to forget your work and labor of love, which ye have shewed toward His name, in that ye have ministered to the saints and do minister.

Foreword

As I began to write this foreword for my husband, I had to reflect back on the steadfast love of God. He is identified all throughout the Bible as the "Master of Giving" from generation to generation.

I praise God that my husband is a man of God. He is valued in our home as God's gift to me and our children, and in the Church as God's gift to the Body of Christ. Living with him daily affords me the opportunity to observe his gentleness, submission to Christ and Godly example. I observe him as he seeks God's face and paves the way for me to be all God created me to be. He has proven his love for God, his family and the wonderful congregation God has given us oversight of.

His dedication to the local church and tireless efforts to advance the cause of Christ cannot go unnoticed. Our partnership together has brought me so much joy and fulfillment. Jesus is the Head of the Church and my husband is the head of our family, my natural example. Because he is free in Christ, he has sought to free so many who have struggled with traditions and the erroneous teachings of our forefathers in the faith.

May you be liberated as you read this powerful revelatory rendition of God's plan for the women called by Him to serve the church of the Lord Jesus Christ. Reverend Flowers' insight is sure to destroy the error and traditional stigma plaguing so many in the Body of Christ.

-Pastor Jacqueline T. Flowers

Introduction

It is <u>not</u> my goal to try to convince anyone, but to share the truth concerning women as truth carriers (Sharers of the Gospel).

For generations God's Word has been on the planet and many people, to this day, have not accepted His Word. Many have set forth a misinterpretation of scripture. So, a book like this is almost unheard of, obsolete, and long overdue.

God said it is my mission to help tear down traditional strongholds. There are many traditions that need to be torn down, such as women should not pastor a church. Satan has perpetrated this lie throughout the earth, so God asked me if I would be a catalyst to spread the truth. My answer was, "Yes."

Advice to the Reader

So God created man in His own image, in the image
of God created He him; male and female created He
them, and God blessed them…
Genesis 1: 27-28 KJV

Before you read this book, ask God to open your
spiritual eyes (insight) to see because a great number
of males and females are trapped in a traditional
mindset. Their eyes have been darkened by the errors
of our ancestors passed down from generation to
generation.

Satan has successfully deceived so many in
the Body of Christ. While some cannot see the
truth, others refuse to accept the truth from God's
perspective. Many will remain blinded by tradition

until they position their hearts to receive spiritual truth and abandon all misinterpretations of scripture. I have studied and researched the Word of God diligently to gain a better understanding of biblical history and the law of scripture interpretation. All scripture must be interpreted in line with what other scriptures say pertaining to the same subject. The Word of God is its own commentary, and is written in harmony with other scriptures to interpret itself. We cannot change the way we think until we change what we know. The question, "Should women preach the gospel?" has been an argument among believers for years. God Himself said,

There is neither Jew nor Greek, there is neither bond nor free, there is neither male nor female: for ye are all one in Christ Jesus.
(Galatians 3:28 KJV)

God is no respecter of persons, but people are still limiting God to the way they feel He should operate instead of embracing His true nature as revealed in His Word. It amazes me how carnal minded some of us can be as Christians. We are so focused on the earth suit (flesh), that we overlook the call of God on many women and blatantly ignore God's power flowing through them. We refuse to receive the Gospel from them. How tragic it is to have missed God because of our own prejudices.

My wife is the pastor of our church. It is a high calling from God, not man. Our Heavenly Father is the only one who can initiate the call. We seem to forget <u>He is God</u> and can use whomever He chooses to preach the Gospel. We must be willing to receive God's Word no matter whom He chooses to speak through. The misinterpretation of scripture that "women cannot preach the Gospel", has to be stopped immediately. As followers of Christ, we must do all we can to stop this error from entering into the next generation and future generations. I believe the world needs to hear this matter addressed by a man of God; not from one on the outside looking in, but from a man whose wife is the pastor and I am proud to say so. I value Pastor Jacqueline T. Flowers as my pastor and my wife. God is doing a mighty work in and through her. I am overjoyed to see her flowing so powerfully in her call and I will continue to do all I can to protect her in the spiritual and natural realm. As Joseph fully accepted the will of God for Mary, the mother of our Lord and Savior Jesus Christ, I fully accept the call of God upon her life and I will not allow anyone or anything to interrupt what God has called her to do. I release her to be all she can be to the Glory of God. God spoke to me concerning His will for her life. He also confirmed the call on her life through me and our pastor.

My prayer is that you will have an open mind and allow God to soften your heart to accept truth as you read this book.

And ye shall know the truth and the truth shall make you free.
(John 8:32 KJV)

What shall we say to these things? If God be for us, who can be against us?
(Romans 8:31 KJV)

I want you to think about this, if we are on God's side, is God for us? Is God on our side when we proclaim the truth? Woman, who can be against you? Preach God's Word.

Chapter 1

Why Write About Women Pastors?

And He must needs go through Samaria.
(John 4:4 KJV)

*I*n the Gospel of John, chapter four, verse four, Jesus defies traditional beliefs and thoughts. Jesus, being a Jew, talking to a Samaritan woman concerning spiritual matters was considered a big no-no! During this time, not to mention out in public also, this was an unbelievable display by the Rabbi Himself. Even the Samaritan woman said to Jesus,

You know Jews have no dealings with the Samaritans.
(John 4:9 KJV)

Many women feel the same way in the 21ˢᵗ century. They feel like Christ shouldn't be talking to them. They feel unneeded and out of place. Jesus answered and said to her,

> *If thou knewest the gift of God...*
> ***(John 4:10 KJV)***

Wow! Isn't this the case in the Body of Christ today concerning women in ministry? Now, let's hold up a bit. I would like to let the readers of this book know that I know that Jesus was asking for a drink of water. Actually, Jesus was asking for a natural thing to communicate a spiritual truth. However, the Samaritan woman could not see spiritually. So, to answer the big question, why write about women pastors? The reasons are:

1. God asked me to help expose and expel a lie that mankind has perpetrated on earth. The lie is that God will not use a woman to pastor in His church.

2. Women also hear from the Lord, but because of false teachings, they doubt the voice of God and His call upon their lives.

Many women can't hear God's voice and His instructions because of either an unhealthy marriage, a misinterpretation of scripture by some die-hard preacher, or family members who think women should be silent in the church. If you are a Minister, Preacher, Doctor, Bishop, Pope or whatever title you have pinned on yourself and you have been teaching this without the correct interpretation, you are demeaning, not helping, the Body of Christ. Please, by all means, read Chapter 4 and be prepared to study the scripture in the Greek. Don't take my word, but honor what the Word of God says.

Why write about women pastors? The truth is truth, no matter who shares the Gospel. Now, let's just think about this for a moment—why listen to any woman if she can't speak the truth in church? Why can she speak the truth in schools? Why did you allow your mother to teach you anything, or why do you think your wife can speak truth to you? This is ridiculous, right? I can go on and on. But you might say, "The woman isn't the head of the church." Well, neither is the man; whether you are a man or a woman you cannot claim lordship of God's church. Many people have misunderstood the scripture. Jesus is the Head of the church, not a man or a woman; <u>JESUS</u>!

And He is the Head of the Body, the Church.
(Colossians 1:18 KJV)

The Church is God's business.

You are all <u>sons</u> (male and female) of God, through faith in Christ Jesus, for all of you who were baptized into Christ have clothed yourselves with Christ. There is neither Jew nor Greek, slave nor free, male nor female, for you are all one in Christ Jesus.
(Galatians 3:26-28 KJV)

I believe Satan has misled many male pastors into believing that God will not use women as pastors. Bad interpretation of the scriptures has always been Satan's method of deceiving people. I pray that mankind, male or female, will 'study to shew thyself approved' (II Timothy 2:15 KJV), and put aside our personal biases and agendas and see the Gospel through God's eyes and not man's view.

Universally, there are more women than men who go to church. Point being, women tend to see more spiritually than men. This is a shocking truth that can't be denied. Don't take my word for it, you judge it. Take a survey. Try looking into ten different states at ten different churches. This book isn't intended to bring the men down, but a book like this is needed for the Body of Christ. We need both male and female pastors to team up against Satan's strategies. As human agents for God on earth, we must not be divided. A divided kingdom cannot stand. This lie that has been perpetrated on earth must stop. God can use women as pastors and He will use whomever He calls, male or female. When God speaks, He can use whatever source He chooses. God used a female donkey to speak.

And the LORD opened the mouth of the donkey, and <u>*she said*</u> *unto Balaam, What have I done unto you, that you have smitten me these three times?*
(Numbers 22:8 KJV)

God used a fish to deliver money for taxes.

Notwithstanding, lest we should offend them, go thou to the sea, and cast an hook, and take up the fish that first cometh up; and when thou hast opened his mouth, thou shalt find a piece of money: that take, and give unto them for me and thee.
(Matthew 17:27 KJV)

God used a raven to feed Elijah.

*The ravens brought him bread and meat in the
morning and bread and meat in the evening, and he
drank from the brook.*
(I Kings 21—17:6 NIV)

God used a rooster to crow at a precise time to
deliver a message to Peter.

*Then he began to call down curses, and he swore to
them, "I don't know the man!" Immediately a rooster
crowed.*
(Matthew 26:74 NIV)

God also used a big fish to get a message across to
Jonah.

*Now the LORD had prepared a great fish to swallow
up Jonah. And Jonah was in the belly of the fish three
days and three nights.*
(Jonah 1:17 KJV)

These examples just give a few ways our Father can
deliver a message to His people. If you are a female
pastor, remember this, stay focused and continue the

work which God called you to do. In the mind of God, He created male and female at the same time (see Genesis 1:27-28 KJV). When God says it, <u>it is done.</u>

Consider Genesis 5:1-2 KJV (emphasis added),

This is the book of the generations of Adam. In the day that God created man, in the likeness of God made He him. Male and female created He them, and blessed them, and called <u>their</u> name <u>Adam</u>, in the day when they were created.

God is no respecter of gender—when God sees male or female, He sees mankind.

Chapter 2

My Wife is the Pastor

*T*here is an old saying that states, "Behind every good man, there is a good woman, and behind every good woman is a good man." Let me say this, God's perspective of man and woman is that they are one. God said the husband and wife are to be one. When God called my wife to pastor, he called me also. When God calls the man to pastor, He also calls the wife to minister. I believe in the order of authority for mankind:

1. God
2. Jesus
3. Holy Spirit
4. Man*kind*

Jerald W. Flowers, Sr.

I believe in the Trinity—God the Father, the Son and the Holy Ghost. When God created man in Genesis 1:27, God created he him; male and female He created them. When you create something you must think of it first. So, in the mind of God, He saw two as one. "Let Us make man (species of mankind) in Our image and likeness" is to say a man and woman's relationship should resemble the Trinity—Father, Son and the Holy Spirit. Basically, man, woman, <u>be holy</u>.

Jesus often said He and the Father are one and God's Word tells us to be Holy as He is Holy. Now what does all this have to do with my wife being the pastor? It is key to know that my wife and I are one. It is okay for her to be called Pastor because she is married and called by God. When God called her, He called me. When you're married, God sees two, not one, with the call. A man and his wife may have different functions, but they have the same call—to win souls for the Kingdom of God, to help set the captives free and mend the broken hearted in the name of Jesus Christ.

My wife struggled with accepting her call as pastor at first because she believed a lie. Her former Pastor told her that God would not use her to pastor. This tradition and many old, traditional and false interpretations of scripture must die out of the minds of people and out of the land today. My wife has been pastoring for over 16 years and God has proven Himself to be faithful in the ministry that she pastors time and time again. She is Pastor and Founder of Time of Celebration Ministries in Houston, Texas. She teaches God's Word with boldness and confidence. She is not intimidated by the persecution of many men and women who are trapped in the carnality of their minds. Remember this, if God is on your side, who can be against you?

Now, a note to the man who is married and your wife has a call on her life to pastor; as a man in this situation, your calling is to humble yourself to God's calling, allowing God to work through whomever He wants to work through. Don't separate yourself spiritually. Remember, your calling is priceless and time sensitive. I love the story in the Gospel of Luke Chapter 1. Picture this; God had a plan to birth a forerunner of Jesus Christ in the earth. Gabriel, the angel that stands in the presence of God, told Zacharias that God wanted to use his wife for the purpose of birthing John the Baptist. This story is an example of what could happen to husbands who doubt God's Word. Because of Zacharias' unbelief, it cost him nine months of being dumb. Men, support your wife. It is better that you shut your mouth and pray before the wrath of God consumes you due to your doubt and unbelief.

When God plans to channel His Word and His Work to His people, wisdom dictates that no one hinder or be a stumbling stone in the way. I would imagine, in the mind of Zacharias, his wife was very old in age; logically, how could she have a child when she was past her season of child bearing years? So, God's insight here for us would be, if you don't understand what God is doing or why He decided to do a work in a specific way, our thoughts should be to trust God, not doubt Him. Get in agreement with His plan and keep in mind that He is the Creator. He can work a plan however or through whomever He chooses.

Our Father God is speaking to us today by more means than man or woman. He has spoken to us in days past by obvious miracles and mankind still struggles to believe in Him. God's decision to use a female pastor is not a great miracle when you consider how he used other aspects of His creation to speak for Him. As I have mentioned earlier, God speaks through any vehicle He chooses. My point here is, we can't put our heavenly Father in a box to suit the way we see things. My wife is the Pastor and I can see it.

Blessed are the pure in heart, for they shall see God.
(Matthew 5:8 KJV)

I was praying on a ship one night, sailing from Alexandria, Egypt. While praying, I looked up and saw the moon and stars shining on a clear, still night. God spoke these words to me, "I am still here." God's Word is spoken to comfort, encourage, direct or rebuke us. No matter what gender speaks the truth, when you are pure in heart, you will see and hear God.

Chapter 3

Female Pastors

<u>Women of the High Calling Confession</u>—*I am God's woman, pressing into the High Calling of God. Because I am the Bride of Christ, I live a life of moral excellence. My life is an expression of the excellence of the Kingdom of God before all men at all times. I think the thoughts of God continuously and speak His Word in every situation. I am God's workmanship. I am not a mistake. I am fearfully and wonderfully made. I conform to the character of God, and I have His authority to operate like Him in the earth. Because the Greater One lives in me, failure is not an option. I am destined to succeed, because I have been fashioned for His Glory, created for His pleasure and empowered to do His Will. I am blessed of the Lord*

and see myself as a woman of value, worthy to be respected, admired and praised. Because my ways please God, He makes my enemies to be at peace with me. I am happy and alert at all times. I am a woman of prayer and refuse to gossip or eat the bread of idleness. I am sound of mind and strong in spirit. I am physically healthy and my Father redeems my life from destruction. He causes everything I set my hands to accomplish to prosper, because my heart is perfect towards Him. I refuse to be jealous, critical or judgmental of others. I walk in love and esteem every member of the Body highly. I see all men through the eyes of God, and therefore, I have the wisdom of God for every situation. I am disciplined and choose to rejoice in the Lord always. I will not leave this earth without making an impact on this generation and on future generations. Because I seek first the Kingdom of God and His Righteousness, there is no lack in my life. I have more than enough to be self-sufficient, having need of nothing and no one. (Written by J.T. Flowers)

<u>As For Me and My House Confession (for men)</u>—
As a man of God, I am the official dignity of God in this earth. I am God's identity. I exemplify the

character and integrity of God. I am God's authority in the earth realm. Christ is my Head and I imitate Him in all that I say and in all that I do. I am a family man; solidified in truth; perfected in righteousness; undefiled by the world. I have an excellent spirit; therefore, I am gentle and kind. I lift up the standard before my family, business associates, friends and neighbors. Therefore, I never need to demand respect; my lifestyle commands the respect I deserve. I am saved, filled with the Holy Spirit and never cease to pray. I am what others must become; therefore, other males are able to extract their behavior from me. My life is hid in Christ and I am not my own. I have been bought with the blood of the Lord Jesus Christ, therefore, I forfeit the right to do as I please. I will not allow myself to be defiled by evil thoughts, sex outside of marriage, drugs, alcohol, cigarettes, pornography, and masturbation, deceit, gambling and such like. I am God's representative in this earth, therefore, success is inevitable and failure is not even an option. I am a servant to my family. I am organized and disciplined; therefore, everything I set my mind to accomplish must prosper. In Jesus name, I am all God created me to be and what I have made up my mind to be. (Written by J.T. Flowers)

I personally believe that God's best plan for a woman with a pastoral high calling is for her to be married. I am very careful in writing this statement. I know that God can do whatever He pleases, but I base this bit of information on the fact that I can't find a scripture to validate an unmarried female as a pastor. God's commission to the Pastor is to feed the church.

Take heed therefore unto yourselves and to all the flock over which the Holy Ghost hath made you overseers, to feed the church of God, which He hath purchased with His own Blood.
(Acts 20:28)

Here is food for thought; When God called Mary, the mother of Jesus to birth Him in the earth, it was a high calling for a woman who was married. Mary was engaged to be married. Being engaged during that time was looked upon as being married. But the fact of the matter is no wedding had taken place.

Now, the birth of Jesus Christ was on this wise, when as His mother Mary was espoused to Joseph, <u>before they came together,</u> she was with child of the Holy Ghost.
(Matthew 1:18 KJV)

Now, what am I saying here? Mary birthed the Word into the earth realm regardless of how you view it. God used this channel to get the Word to mankind. Let's look at another situation in the Bible concerning Eve, the first woman on earth. Satan, through Eve, ushered in the fall of mankind on the earth. I realize that here, we have two completely opposite cases. In both cases, it shows an everlasting impact that the female had on this planet, be it negative or positive.

But I would have you know, that the head of every man is Christ and the head of the woman is man; and the head of Christ is God.
(I Corinthians 11:3 KJV)

In verses 4-9 in the 11th chapter of Corinthians, we see a Jewish traditional mindset that is looked at in a literal sense (meaning the woman has to have her head covered physically). Jews practice this tradition today. The spiritual parallel is seen in verse 10,

For this cause ought the woman to have power (authority) on her head because of the angels (demonic activity).

So, to say this in a way the reader will understand, a woman must have regulations and be governed, or ruled by her head (meaning her husband) because of the spiritual covering needed to ward off evil spiritual attacks (demons).

In this book, I will not attempt to explain everything in grave detail. It is my plan to write a sequel because there is so much information to discuss.

A misinterpretation of scripture is a trick of the enemy to try to poison the minds of thousands of strong believers (male and female) against women pastors. I cannot find a scripture that forbids women from preaching. I think one of the biggest mistakes female pastors make is trying to mimic male pastors in their delivery of the Word. If you were born female, be a lady. The anointing is on the Word, not the style.

God is no respecter of persons. But in every nation he that feareth Him, and worketh righteousness, is accepted with God.
(Acts 10:34 KJV)

Another common mistake many female pastors make is constantly apologizing that they are female.

<u>Just be who you are</u>. Your gender is not important to a serious Christian who is seeking the truth from God's Word. In a court of law, it is not an issue whether you are a female or male. Just like a female attorney never mentions the fact that she is a female, female pastors should model the same behavior. The congregation wants truth, not an announcement that you are female. Just trust God's Word. Remember this, "If God be for us, who can be against us?" (Romans 8:31b KJV) This passage is our key to it all.

Many females allow their husbands to make them a pastor. After being a Christian for many years, I have noticed in the Body of Christ that if a husband is the pastor of the church, he would elevate himself to Bishop, and then promote his wife from 'First Lady' to 'Co-Pastor' or 'Pastor'. If you were called into the pastorate by your husband and not God, I think you should seriously question your calling. Because the husband is the head of the wife and God will not violate His authority, God will get permission from the husband to use the wife. Many organizations license and ordain women to preach, pastor, and teach the Word. Your calling should be undeniable with signs following. God should be showing Himself strong in the ministry. I am not saying that your call is not a valid call if your husband, the pastor, promoted you to pastor; what I am saying is that many male pastors promote themselves to a higher call, not ordained by God, and they feel obligated to elevate their wife to the office of a pastor. You should be certain that your calling is sure and not an agenda from your husband, the pastor.

I believe that titles in the Body of Christ today can be misleading. So many people ask themselves the question, "What am I?" Many females get caught in the same traps as it relates to their title. We see in Judges 4:4-5 and Judges 5:13 that Deborah was a judge for both civil and criminal cases. The children of Israel came to her for judgment. She was a married woman and the chief ruler of Israel for 40 years, giving orders to the generals and all the army. She did the work of an evangelist, prophetess, judge and preacher. God gave her authority over the mighty nation of Israel. Whether you call yourself a prophetess, pastor, evangelist, preacher, bishop, or whatever, the key is to have God on your side and minister His Word with faith and power.

This book would be too large if I attempted to write about every female in the bible who God used to minister His Word. The Bible tells us in Micah 6:4 KJV, Miriam was a prophetess and song leader in

Israel. Huldah was another powerful woman of God. Five men went to Huldah and communed with her in 2 Kings 22:14 KJV. She spoke to a congregation of men concerning the book of the law. A female pastor preached to a congregation of men, imagine that! In the New Testament, we have Phoebe, another woman of God who Paul himself commended. In fact she assisted Paul in his work for the Lord. If you research Romans 16:12, Phoebe is described as a servant of the church. In fact, this scripture helps me out when the enemy attacks my mind about the female pastor. I actually dissected <u>this verse in the Greek</u> and found out that word 'servant' indicates that Phoebe was a pastor. Let's look at it, Paul wrote (emphasis added),

*I commend unto you Phoebe, our sister, which is **servant** of the church which is at Cenchrea.*
(Romans 16:1 KJV)

The King James translation of the word, 'servant' must be looked at in depth to understand the true meaning of what Paul wrote. In Greek, the word, "servant" is "Diakonos" which means to be a teacher and pastor; a deacon or deaconess; minister, to serve. So, Paul wrote that Phoebe was the pastor of the church which was in Cenchrea. Some want to say she was a deaconess, but you do not bestow this type of honor upon a deaconess. Now if you have a problem with this, you have a problem with God. If your heart is corrupt, you won't be able to see. You will continue to view every statement of truth from a shallow perspective. For example, every place you see the word, 'man' in the bible, you won't be able to see that God is addressing man*kind* because in many passages the Bible speaks generically. Another example is in Proverbs 22:6 KJV (emphasis added),

*Train up a child in the way **he** should go and when **he** is old **he** will not depart from it.*
(Proverbs 22:6 KJV)

Now test your depth of insight; is God telling us that only men will not depart from it? The word 'he' in this passage is inclusive of the female gender, is it not? If you feed a small thinker, they will interpret it as only addressing the male seed and not mankind. Here is another example in Matthew,

Then said Jesus unto His disciples, if any man will come after Me, let him deny himself, and take up his cross and follow Me.
(Matthew 16:24 KJV)

Now you tell me, is this passage addressing the male man or mankind? Mankind means males and females. So, if you have a narrow mind and a corrupt heart, it really won't matter to you whether I explain it to you or you see it for yourself in the Word of God. The bible states in Matthew 5:8 KJV,

Blessed are the pure in heart for they shall see God.
(Matthew 5:8)

To the female pastors, know this; there will always be critics around. If you are truly called by God, just stand on God's Word—always stay focused and preach the Word. Preach like you know who you are and not a whooping entertainer. Remember, Romans 8:31 (KJV) states, "If God be for us, who can be against us?" The Dragon (Satan) has been after the woman to draw an abundance of people from the truth.

And the dragon stood before the woman, which was ready to be delivered, for to devour her child as soon as it was born.
(Revelation 12:4 KJV)

It's unfortunate that Satan is still holding a grudge against the woman, especially female pastors, to stop them from talking about the kingdom of Christ. I strongly encourage you to study Revelations Chapter 12. God made provision and protection for the woman (Revelation 12:6 KJV) and God is still providing for His church today. In Revelation Chapter 12, the woman is described in celestial images. Let's look into this revelation—the spiritual always comes before the natural. You can see one example in Genesis 1:26 KJV when God said;

Let Us make man in Our Image after Our Likeness.
(Genesis 1:26 KJV)

You see, God *created* in this passage the spiritual; but He <u>formed</u> man, which is natural, in Genesis 2:7.

Let's get back to the woman in Revelation Chapter 12—we see what happened in the spirit, so I will break it down in simpler terms. This is the first sign that John references and it is described as a great sign. Note that in Revelation Chapters 12, 13, and 14, figures of the Great Tribulation are described and this great sign introduces the first seven. (Follow me and this will all make sense shortly). One, the woman represents Israel or the Church. Secondly, the 'dragon' represents Satan and evil. Lastly, the "man child" refers to Jesus Christ. I won't get into the other four signs because it would take us too far away from the subject matter. The woman represents a religious system, as the Bride of Christ (associated with the Church, Revelation Chapter 19:7-8). Here is the summary; the dragon chases the woman because the woman has the Word, which is Jesus. So Satan and his demons hate the woman because she reminds him of his ultimate defeat—**Jesus Christ**. The dragon spirit, which is pure evil, wants to shut everyone down who will deliver the Word, especially the woman. The woman was the channel God used to bring Jesus into the earth. It is clear that Jesus is to rule all nations with a rod of iron (see Revelation Chapter 12:5). There is much more to say about this great sign, but my point is to share the hidden mystery as to why there are so many people against female pastors. The dragon spirit is influencing many and is very much alive today. But, when you are on God's side, no one can be against you.

I don't intend to be 'deep' in this book, but it is really important for the female pastor to understand why Satan hates you so much. You have to get the revelation concerning the dragon and the woman. God used the woman to birth Jesus, the man child, or the Word, into the earth. So every time you proclaim the Gospel in your church, it is a reminder to Satan of when he got kicked out of heaven. Satan drew the third part of the stars (angels) of heaven. God cast them out of Heaven with Satan. So, there you have a glimpse of the picture of what happened and why you as a female pastor, have so many people that are against you.

He that is not with Me is against Me and he that gathered not with Me, scattereth abroad.
(Matthew 12:30 KJV)

The people who are against you are against Christ. But keep this passage in mind,

When the enemy shall come in like a flood, the Spirit of the Lord shall lift up a standard against him.
(Isaiah 59:19 KJV)

Don't try to throw a rock at every barking dog. Just stay focused, stand on God's Word, stay pure, and know that you are truly called. If you are not sure, remain under the authority of your Pastor, and be still until you know without a doubt what God has called you to do and you can't fail. God will confirm the call.

Chapter 4

Women Being Silent in the Church

Let your women keep silence in the churches: for it is not permitted unto them to speak, but they are commanded to be under obedience, as also saith the law. And if they will learn anything, let them ask their husbands at home, for it is a shame for women to speak in the church.
I Corinthians 14:34-35 KJV

The Word of God instructs us to study to show ourselves approved, and the above verses have definitely been misinterpreted for generations by pastors, preachers and just plain old church folk. Even the heathen in the streets will quote these scriptures, but the sad thing about this is people really believe in their hearts that they have the correct interpretation. I searched through several bible translations trying to find one that will do justice with regards to this passage. The words in the Message Bible say,

Wives must not disrupt worship, talking when they should be listening, asking questions that could more appropriately be asked of their husbands at home. God's Book of the law guides our manners and customs here. Wives have no license to use the time of worship for unwarranted speaking.
(I Corinthians 14:34-35 MSG)

Now, if you study the word "women" in verse 34, in Greek, this word is 'yuv'n' (translation 'gyne' which means 'wife'); so the interpretation here would be that Paul, the writer, is setting the proper order of worship, being certain that wives were speaking out in church causing confusion (as a child in a classroom who does not fully understand the lesson and blurts out the wrong answers). The wives were out of order and did not have the approval of their husbands, so the correct way to say this would be (emphasis added),

Let your wife be peaceful in the churches, for it is not permitted unto them to speak, but they are commanded to be subject under as also saith, the moral instruction given by Christ.

I Corinthians 14:35 is not a commandment from God for women not to speak in the church, but to a select group of married women who were letting their emotions rule their behavior instead of getting approval from their husbands to speak so all things would be done decently and in order. Note that every woman doesn't have a husband, so this could not be a mandate for all women. There is no sound reason why a female should not pastor or preach the good news of Christ. In fact, there is a desperate need in the church for more workers. I don't believe it is a mandate from God for the single female to be married in ministry, but it sure would make matters easier if a strong Godly man was by her side to take some of the heat off of her.

One of the problems you may have as a female pastor is controlling your emotions. Most women have a time in their life where they go through a hormonal imbalance, and a man who is not intimidated by the female, as pastor, can help regulate her thoughts. All I am saying here is two is better than one.

I strongly encourage the female Pastor to wear a robe or appropriate attire during the delivery of the Word. It would be best if she uses discretion. The congregation doesn't need to be distracted by her physical anatomy. The intentions should be for the church to focus on the Word of God and not her body. In addition to that, the female pastor should not be overweight. The people will shy away from you because they will see you as a person who lacks discipline. We have actually had people to say they can't receive from a 'fat' pastor, and as a female pastor, believe me, when I say you will have enough opposition coming against you, so don't add more to your battle.

Now, let me get back to the scriptures. Many preachers who pastor don't have the correct interpretation of I Corinthians 14:34-35. You will notice your greatest opposition will come from within the Body of Christ because Satan really wants the Body fighting against itself, then he can sit back and watch the church self-destruct. Let's dissect another interesting sounding passage from the scripture.

But I suffer not a woman to teach, nor to usurp authority over the man, but to be in silence.
(I Timothy 2:12 KJV)

Scriptures like this one and the one in I Corinthians 14:34-35 can wreak havoc in the mind of a woman if she is called to preach. It is very sad that many well known pastors, bishops and even other women have been indoctrinated to believe that a female cannot teach God's Word. If you don't study the Word, you can definitely be led to believe a lie. Here is the correct interpretation of I Timothy 2:12 from the Greek mind (emphasis added),

> ***But I will not permit the wife to govern or exercise dominion over her husband, but to be peaceful.***

I am no great theologian or some kind of genius, but the Word will speak for itself <u>if we study.</u> God is not trying to bar all women from speaking in church. If women are not allowed to speak in the church, why allow them to sing, pray, teach a class, make announcements, etc? It really sounds ridiculous when you stop and think about it. Would you allow a woman to testify for you in a court room? Just answer that for yourself. Think about this, can a woman tell the truth? What about your mother, sister, aunt or that female doctor, or a grade school teacher or any woman who has given you instruction. How ridiculous! The bottom line is anyone can tell the truth. Every man or woman is entitled to believe what he or she chooses to believe, but God's Word will stand long after we are gone. When you or I, or whoever reads this book dies, God's Word will still be standing.

There is neither Jew nor Greek, there is neither bond nor free. There is neither male nor female, for ye are all one in Christ Jesus.
(Galatians 3:28 KJV)

The Body of Christ needs laborers to preach the Gospel regardless of whether they are male or female. God will use whomever He chooses.

Chapter 5

My Testimony

*M*y wife is my pastor and has been for the past 16 years. During this period of my life, I have witnessed very distasteful acts from male pastors to first ladies, men and women in the congregations, and even strange behavior from some relatives. It is very clear to me that Satan wants my wife to shut up and quit. But I have been a strong arm for her to lean on. I've never had to demand respect from her or the congregation. My lifestyle commands the respect I deserve. I reiterate that God said this to me one day, "Mankind has perpetrated a lie on the planet that says I will not use a woman, will you help Me?" I vowed to God that I would be there to help prove that He is no respecter of gender, and God has proven to us throughout the many years that He is with us. I had people try to belittle me for taking this kind of stand. I have had many mental battles engineered by Satan to get me off course from this walk as the man who allows his wife to pastor. Men, if your wife is called to preach, don't stand in the way—you are in direct opposition to God and God will deal with you. I have trusted God first and my pastor and I know of couples who have tried to pastor without God and failed by divorcing or by the early death of the male man. God has blessed our marriage of 27 years and we are still going strong. He has blessed the church He has placed us as stewards over. Many male pastors get it twisted as it pertains to who is the head of the church. My wife and I have always acknowledged Jesus as the Head of the church and we are spreading His Word. I know many pastors will stand behind the pulpit and declare that they are the head of the church, but my Bible states,

Christ is the Head of the church.
(Ephesians 5:23 KJV)

And He is the Head of the Body, the Church; Who is the beginning, the firstborn from the dead; that in all things He might have preeminence.
(Colossians 1:18 KJV)

I believe Jesus knows how to run His church.

Men, if you are in a church where your wife is the pastor, your job as the head of your wife is to fight spiritually and be an example for the Body of Christ and to take notice that Christ will use any vessel He desires to use. Never disagree with your wife in front of the church. Be pure, be humble, be understanding, and be all you can be to help God use her. You must fight the spirit of jealousy and competition. Many times you will feel unimportant. People will watch you to determine what kind of relationship you have with your wife, the pastor. You should pray for the congregation often because the enemy doesn't want anyone to hear the Gospel from a female pastor. Don't underestimate or belittle the importance of your role as the pastor's husband. I am a very active part of the ministry at Time of Celebration Ministries Church and am responsible for many duties as the pastor's husband. I am the Director of the Music Ministry and Men's Ministry. I am also the head of the Audio/Visual Ministry.

God enables me to teach His Word with conviction, simplicity and unwavering faith. My wife and I share in counseling sessions, marriage enrichment, hospital and prison visitations. I'm in charge of the baptismal services and I oversee almost every aspect of ministry in our local church. I can't do everything, but when things go wrong, I must know how to correct it. My duties are endless from emptying the trash to unstopping the toilets, etc. I can go on and on, but I have only named a few things. My point is this, if you take care of God's business, He will, without a shadow of a doubt, take care of your business. I truly enjoy working for God in our church and I don't have a problem with my wife being my Pastor. I realize that this is a move of God and everybody can't discern when God is moving. Time of Celebration Ministries Church in Houston, Texas is not a church for everyone because if God wants it said, we say it regardless of what the end result will be. The Word of God is taught at our church unapologetically and with clarity and boldness. We strongly believe that God's Word should not only bring healing, encouragement and comfort, but it should also convict and provoke change. God's mighty Hand is upon our church and He continues to be glorified through this ministry.

I pray that this book will make a difference in the Body of Christ. I know I will be persecuted for taking a stand, but my aim is to please God, not man. I originally planned to write seven chapters but I underestimated how much work is involved in writing a book and putting my thoughts on paper. This is another assignment the Lord gave me. There is much more I could have shared in this book, but this is just a start. If God allows me to, I will do a sequel to this book to totally complete it.

Lastly, to all female pastors, (or those women who are just realizing they are called to pastor), it is not an easy task to pastor a church as a woman. Continue to press forward, be humble, stay focused and remain God centered. You are a servant of the Most High, our Lord and Savior Jesus Christ. Your divine purpose is to be Christ-like and persistently work to multiply Christ in others. When you come against opposition, always remember, if God be for you, who can be against you?

To be continued...

About the Author

Rev. J. W. Flowers, Sr. is the multi-talented Elder and oversight Pastor of Time of Celebration Ministries Church in Houston, Texas. He is committed to upholding the standard of character, ethics, and integrity. Rev. Flowers is the Director of the Music Ministry and the creative head of the Audio/Media Ministry and the Men's Ministry. Along with his wife, he oversees counseling, marriage enrichment, Ordinance Ministry and the teaching of God's Word. He graduated from college with an Associates Degree in Music, and is the producer of several albums. He ministers the Word of God boldly and is a vivid demonstration before the people of God as a man of discipline, prayer and sound spiritual conviction. He shares with the men of God that God is not a respecter of persons and has not restricted Himself to the male gender. Reverend Flowers states, "God will use whomever He chooses to proclaim the truth of His Word." Rev. Flowers is determined to see his wife preach the gospel alongside him. Together, their boldness, team effort and Godly example are impacting both men and women!

www.ingramcontent.com/pod-product-compliance
Lightning Source LLC
Chambersburg PA
CBHW021225020426
42331CB00003B/470